READY, SET, DRAW!

COOL BOY STUFF YOU CAN DRAW

Nicole Brecke

Patricia M. Stockland

Millbrook Press / Minneapolis

The images in this book are used with the permission of: © iStockphoto.com/Dzianis Miraniuk, p. 4; © iStockphoto.com, pp. 4, 5; © iStockphoto.com/Boris Yankov, p. 5; © iStockphoto.com/JR Trice, p. 5; © iStockphoto.com/Temelko Temelkov, p. 7; © iStockphoto.com/Joe Gough, p. 9; © iStockphoto.com/Aleksander Bolbot, p. 11; © iStockphoto.com/Richard Laurence, pp. 14–15; © iStockphoto.com/Denis Jr. Tangney, pp. 18–19; © iStockphoto.com/George Argyropoulos, pp. 22–23; © iStockphoto.com/Nick M. Do, pp. 26–27; © iStockphoto.com/Jarno Gonzalez Zarraonandia, pp. 30–31.

Front cover: © iStockphoto.com/Richard Laurence, (city); © iStockphoto.com/Temelko Temelkov, (forest); © iStockphoto.com/blackred (hand).

Edited by Mari Kesselring
Research by Emily Temple

Text and illustrations copyright © 2010 by Lerner Publishing Group, Inc.

Millbrook Press
A division of Lerner Publishing Group, Inc.
241 First Avenue North
Minneapolis, MN 55401 U.S.A.

Website address: www.lernerbooks.com

Library of Congress Cataloging-in-Publication Data

Brecke, Nicole.
        Cool boy stuff you can draw / by Nicole Brecke and Patricia M. Stockland ; illustrations by
    Nicole Brecke.
                p.   cm. — (Ready, set, draw!)
        Includes index.
        ISBN: 978–0–7613–4163–5 (lib. bdg. : alk. paper)
        1. Drawing—Technique—Juvenile literature. I. Stockland, Patricia M. II. Title.
    NC655.B74 2010
    743—dc22   2009004598

Manufactured in the United States of America
1 2 3 4 5 6 – BP – 15 14 13 12 11 10

TABLE OF CONTENTS

ABOUT THIS BOOK

Monsters, heroes, and sports pros! This collection of boy stuff is just for you. With the help of this book, you can start sketching your favorite things. Color a dragon. Or draw a skateboarder. Soon you'll know how to draw many types of cool creatures and people.

Follow these steps to create each character. Each drawing begins with a basic form. The form is made up of a line and a shape or two. These lines and shapes will help you make your drawing the correct size.

A First, read all the steps and look at the pictures. Then use a pencil to lightly draw the line and shapes shown in RED. You will erase these lines later.

B Next, draw the lines shown in BLUE.

C Keep going! Once you have completed a step, the color of the line changes to BLACK. Follow the BLUE line until you're done.

WHAT YOU WILL NEED

PENCIL SHARPENER

COLORED PENCILS

HELPFUL HINTS

Be creative. Use your imagination. Read about your favorite creature, superhero, or sports pro. Then follow the steps to sketch your own book of cool things.

Practice drawing different lines and shapes. All your drawings will start with these.

Use very light pencil lines when you are drawing.

Helpful tips and hints will offer you good ideas on making the most of your sketch.

Colors are exciting. Try to use a variety of shades. This will add value, or depth, to your finished drawings.

Keep practicing, and have fun!

ERASER

PENCIL

PAPER

HOW TO DRAW AN OGRE

The most famous ogre you know might be
Shrek. But ogres have been part of fairy-tale lore for a
long time. Some ogres are trolls, while others are based on
cyclops. Cyclops was a one-eyed giant in Greek and Roman
mythology (a collection of beliefs and stories). What does the
ogre in your mind look like? Is it ugly? Huge? Strong? Can it
turn people into stone? Maybe your ogre lives in a cave. Use
your imagination to create this monster and its hiding place.

1 Lightly draw a small
base oval. Add a
straight center line.
Draw a large, wide
oval starting at the
bottom of the line.

2 Draw a head with a
square, bumpy jaw.
Add two small, pointy
triangles for ears. Add
large arms along the
outside of the big oval.

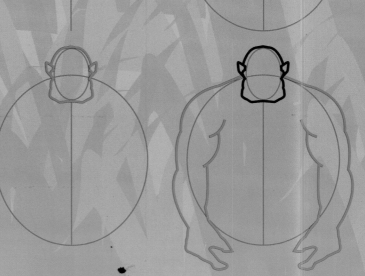

3

Make two short horizontal lines for the chest and a semicircle for the belly. Draw a rough, wide **V** and two small lines for the shorts.

4

Add legs and six small circles for toes. Carefully erase your base shapes and line. Add eyes, a nose, a mouth, and a belly button.

5

Now it's time to color your ogre!

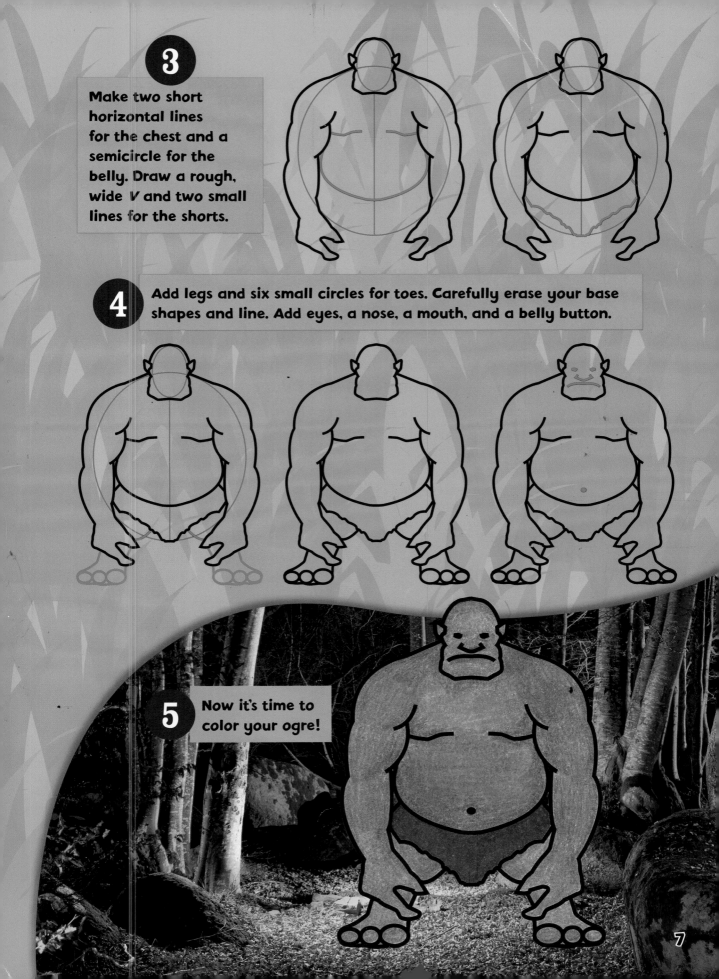

HOW TO DRAW A GIANT

Mighty and large. A titan of the underworld. Builders of mountains. Giants can be any of these things. And in many different stories, giants have superhuman strength. Giants were said to control the forces of nature. Giants created the mountains and carried the sky on their shoulders. Perhaps your giant does all of these things. He can live in the clouds. Or he can rule the ocean. Make sure your giant is big—and strong!

1 Lightly draw a small base oval and a long center line. Add long hair and a beard.

2 Draw an arm using two slightly curved vertical lines. Join them to form a hand at the end. Add the side and waist. Repeat this for the other side.

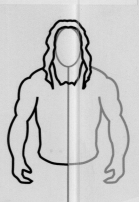

3

Make two small lines for the chest. Add a belly button. Draw four vertical lines for the pants. Make two ragged lines to finish them. Add calves and feet.

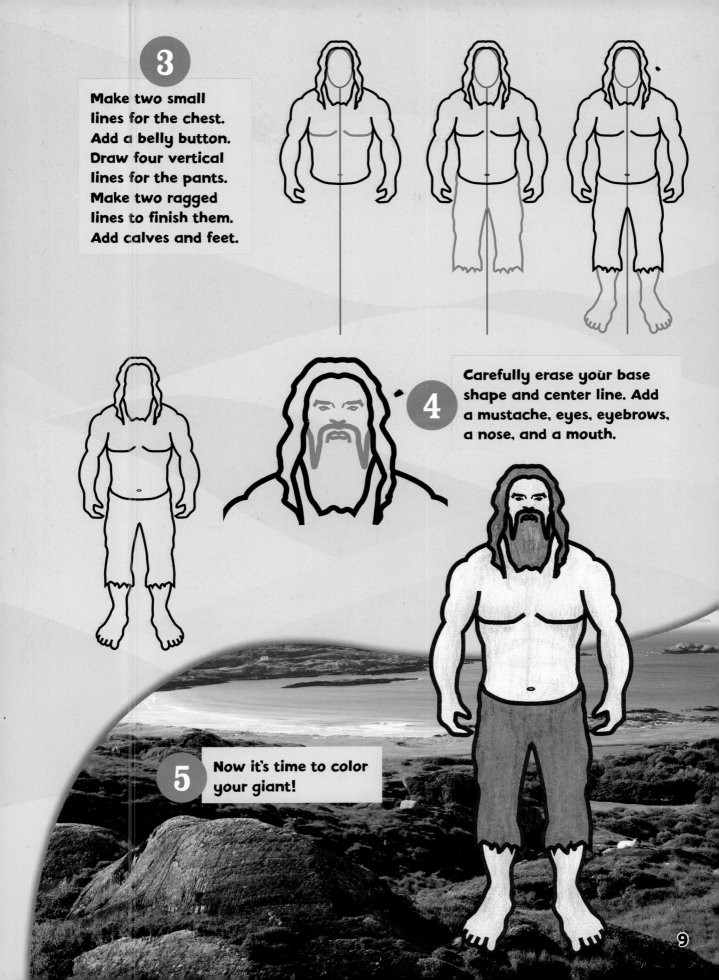

4 Carefully erase your base shape and center line. Add a mustache, eyes, eyebrows, a nose, and a mouth.

5 Now it's time to color your giant!

HOW TO DRAW A DRAGON

Many legends exist about dragons. These fire-breathing creatures can fly through the sky, sleep underwater, and protect hidden treasures. Mythical dragons are sometimes dangerous. Other times, they are protectors—or pets. Dragons might be the enemies of dragon slayers (fighters). Or dragons might be symbols of change. Decide whether your dragon will have wings. How many claws does it have? Three? Four? Five? Or more? Is it a dangerous dragon or a peaceful protector?

1 Draw a light, small base circle. Add a curving line. Make the muzzle and front of the neck.

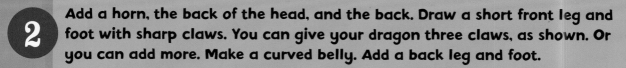

2 Add a horn, the back of the head, and the back. Draw a short front leg and foot with sharp claws. You can give your dragon three claws, as shown. Or you can add more. Make a curved belly. Add a back leg and foot.

3

Draw a long, curved tail with a triangle tip. Add a rounded wing.

4

Carefully erase your center line and base shape. Add two curved lines to the wing. Add an eye and a nostril.

5 Now it's time to color your dragon!

HOW TO DRAW A SUPERHERO

Superheroes are ready to leap into action when danger strikes. Superman was the first well-known superhero. He arrived in the 1930s to help save the world from evil. Soon after that, other superheroes hit the comic-book scene. Batman, Spider-Man, the Fantastic Four, Iron Man, and others showed off their special skills at fighting villains. Superpowers and special abilities make each hero unique. Some have superhuman strength. Others can fly. What can your superhero do?

1 Draw a small base oval. Add a slightly bent center line. Draw the top of the head, the back of the neck, and the tricep.

2 Draw the shorts. Add a bent leg and a tall boot. Draw the other leg straight, with a pointed boot.

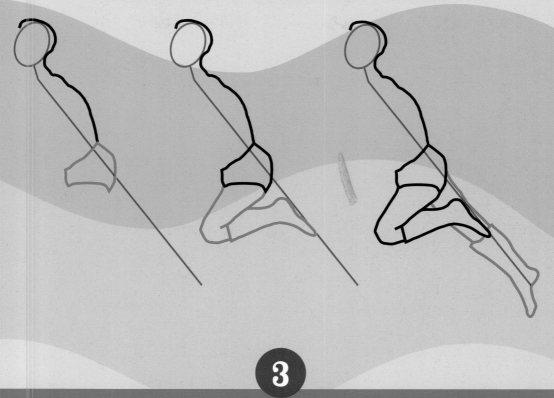

3

Draw a small beltline above the shorts. Make a gloved fist. Add diagonal lines for the stomach, chest, and bicep. Add two more diagonal lines and a gloved fist for the extended arm. Add a forehead, nose, jaw, and neckline.

4 Carefully erase your baseline and shape.

5 Add a long cape.

CLEVER DISGUISE

Superheroes need to keep their true identities a secret.

DRAW A MASK!

A

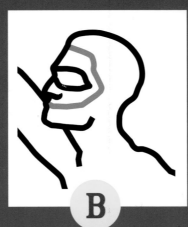

B

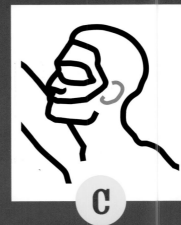

C

When superheros work as a team, their powers against evil are even stronger.

6 Now it's time to color your superhero!

HOW TO DRAW A VILLAIN

Bad guys can be just as exciting as good guys. And for every superhero, there's an archrival—or villain. The Green Goblin, the Joker, the Riddler, and others have all challenged famous superheroes. Villains always have a variety of weapons and tricks. They are sneaky, evil, no-good characters. Your villain might have lots of telltale traits. Arched eyebrows or a battle scar. A giant humpback or a twisted, evil grin. Make your villain battle worthy. Then sketch a creepy backdrop for your bad guy!

1 Draw a narrow base oval and a center line. Add two bent lines from the end of the center line. Draw the head and one ear.

2

Make the body of the coat. Add a longer, closed sleeve and a shorter, open sleeve. Add a hand to the closed sleeve. Draw a gloved fist on the open sleeve.

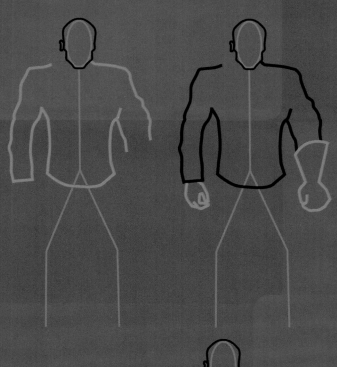

3

Draw a longer pant leg on one side and a shorter leg on the other side. Add a short boot and a taller boot.

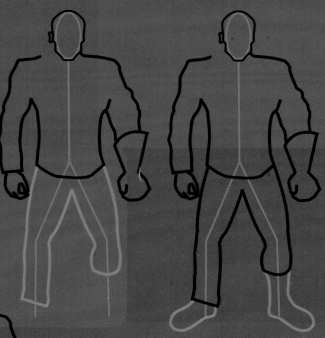

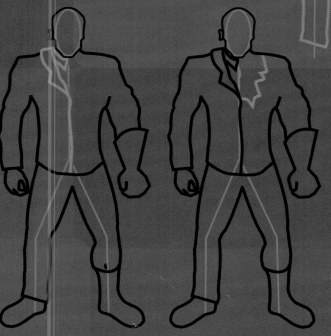

4

Use zigzag lines for the coat collar. Draw two small diagonal lines and a vertical line for the shirt collar. Make a vertical jacket seam. Add a middle line and a jagged line to form a torn shirt.

5 Before finishing the face, carefully erase your base shape, center line, and bent lines.

6 Draw a vertical line in the center of the face. Add a bent horizontal mouth line to the bottom. Add a second line above this for the nose and scar. Make a third horizontal line for the brow. Draw a small eye underneath. Add an eye patch circle. Add two more scar lines.

Did you know...

THE GOAL OF A VILLAIN IS TO DESTROY HIS OWN CITY OR TO CONQUER A SUPERHERO.

Many classic villains were once good and then became criminals.

7 Now it's time to color your villain!

HOW TO DRAW A BASEBALL PLAYER

People around the world are passionate about baseball. The sport has been popular in the United States since the late 1800s. Thirty teams compete in the Major Leagues. So you have plenty of places to find a favorite player. Baseball players need batting, fielding, and throwing skills. And they need to be smart and quick on their feet. Baseball players use safety equipment such as batting helmets and shin guards. But they also use their brains. Baseball is about strategy as well as athletic skills.

1 Draw a base circle. Add a bent center line. Starting from the angled point, add another bent line. Draw a helmet and brim.

2 Make the back and bottom of the jersey. Add a short sleeve. Draw an arm and gloved fist. Add the other sleeve, arm, and glove lines.

3 Follow the bent line on the right side to draw the player's back leg. Follow the straight line on the left side to draw the other leg. Draw a line at the bottom of each leg to make pant cuffs. Add a belt at the waist.

4 Draw shoes at the end of each leg. Add details for soles and laces.

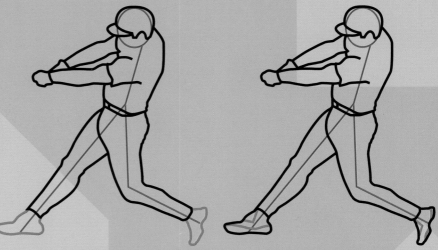

5 Carefully erase your base shape and lines. Draw a profile, jaw, shirt collar, and ear.

6 Follow the leg lines to add seams. Draw a bat extending from the fists.

BATTER UP

If you're going to play baseball, you'll need a ball.

DRAW A BASEBALL!

A.

B.

C.

7 Now it's time to color your baseball player!

MODERN BASEBALLS are hard and hold their shape. But in the early years of baseball, the balls quickly became squishy and had to be replaced.

23

HOW TO DRAW A
FOOTBALL
PLAYER

The first official football rules were written in 1876. Since then, football has grown to be one of the most popular sports in the United States. Professional, college, high-school, and grade-school players all take the field each season with energy and enthusiasm. Your favorite player might be a pro or someone you know. Think about your favorite team and plays. Then create your own Most Valuable Player. Your player can take control as quarterback. Or he can crush the offense with his amazing tackling skills!

1

Draw a small base oval. Add a center line with three angles. Make a helmet around the oval. Add a shoulder, collar, and neckline.

2 Draw the back of the thigh. Add the calf and foot. Draw the shin and top of the shoe.

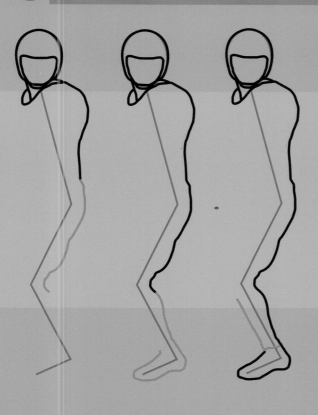

3 Add the back shoe and shin. Draw the front of the forward leg.

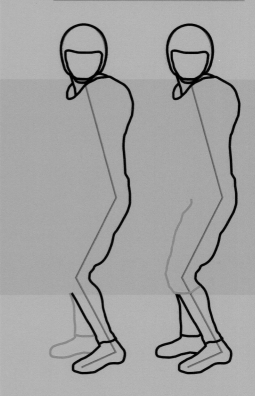

4 Draw the back leg and center seam. Make the waistline and front of the jersey. Add two lines to the side of the pant leg.

5

Make a short sleeve near the shoulder. Add a bent front arm, four fingers, and the back shoulder. Draw the back elbow and the football. Add four more fingers.

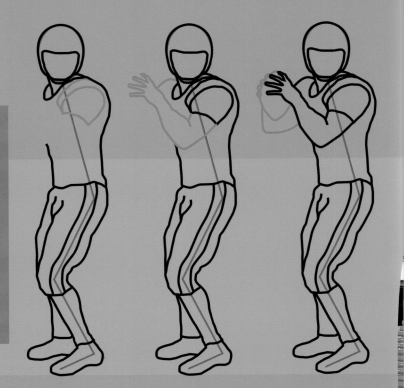

6

Erase your baseline and shape. Add a face mask to the bottom of the helmet and a rectangle to the front of the helmet. Add eyes and a nose.

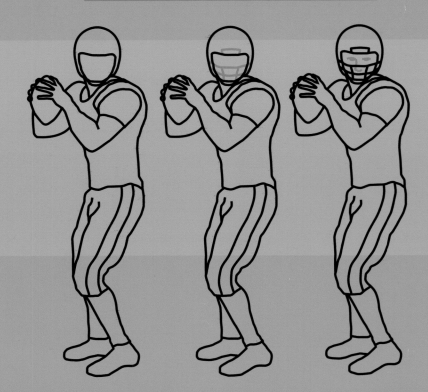

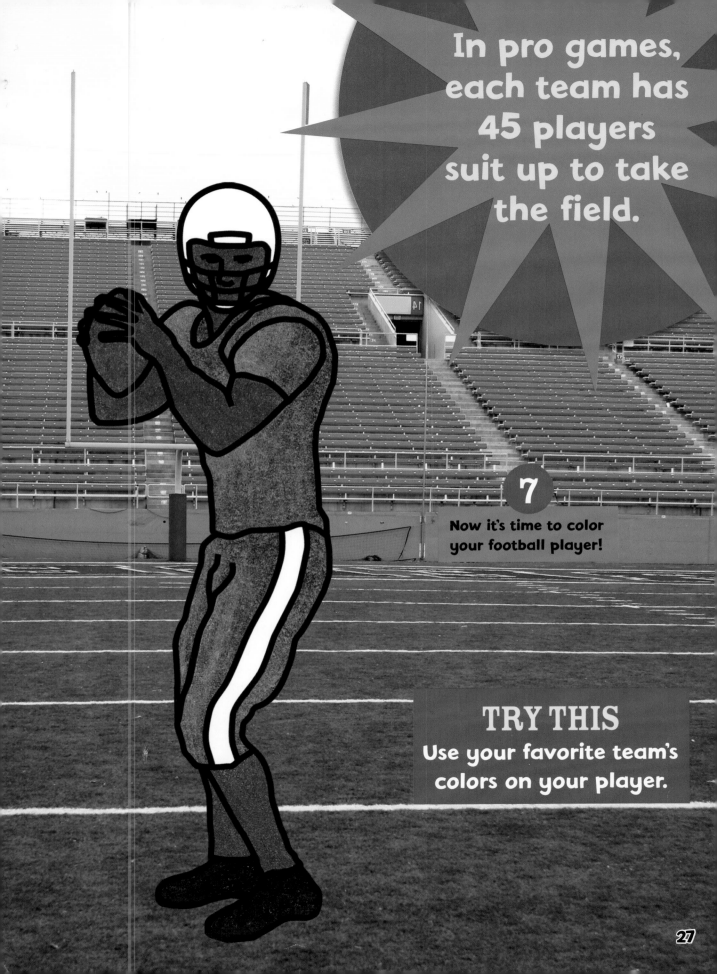

In pro games, each team has 45 players suit up to take the field.

7

Now it's time to color your football player!

TRY THIS
Use your favorite team's colors on your player.

HOW TO DRAW A SKATEBOARDER

Skateboards wouldn't be here without roller skates and surfboards. Sound crazy? Think again! Skateboarding was invented when some surfers got the idea to add roller-skate wheels to their boards. The idea took off! Soon many people were trying it. Some famous skateboarders include Tony Hawk, Bob Burnquist, and Shaun White. These guys have excellent moves, dangerous skills, and intense imaginations. Does your favorite skateboarder work the half-pipe? Or does he work the skate parks? Create a grinding, jumping legend of your own.

 1 Draw two small, overlapping base ovals. Add two diagonal baselines.

2 Outline the top oval for the helmet. Add a chin strap and the jawline.

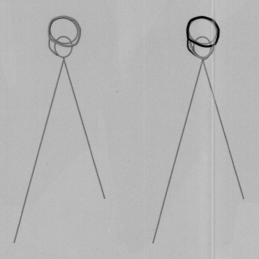

3 Draw a short-sleeved shirt with an angled hem. Add a collar line. Make an arm and fist from one sleeve. Add a bent arm and hand from the other.

4 Using the baselines as guides, draw each pant leg. Add a cross shape for the center seams. Draw two shoes. Add details for soles and laces.

Fast Fact...
SKATEBOARDING TRICKS HAVE AWESOME NAMES, SUCH AS KICK TURN, THE NO COMPLY, AND McTWIST.

5 Carefully erase your base shapes and lines.

6 Draw two small horizontal lines for each eye and eyebrow. Add two more small lines for the nose and mouth.

WICKED RIDE

Your skateboarder will need a skateboard to hit the half-pipe.

DRAW A SKATEBOARD!

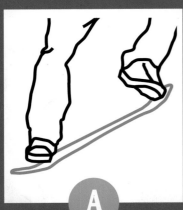

A

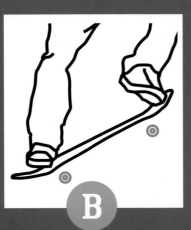

B

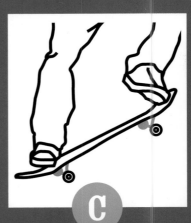

C

Draw stickers on your skateboarder's helmet.

7 Now it's time to color your skateboarder!

FURTHER READING

Animal Planet: Dragons
http://animal.discovery.com/convergence/dragons

Aronson, Marc, and HP Newquist. *For Boys Only: The Biggest, Baddest Book Ever*.
    New York: Feiwel and Friends, 2007.

Brecke, Nicole, and Patricia M. Stockland. *Cars, Trucks, and Motorcycles You Can Draw*.
    Minneapolis: Millbrook Press, 2010.

Buller, Laura, and Tim Hammond. *Sports*. New York: DK Publishing, 2006.

DC HeroZone
http://dcherozone.kidswb.com/games#/GreenArrow.swf

Knudsen, Shannon. *Giants, Trolls, and Ogres*. Minneapolis: Lerner Publications Company, 2010.

Sports Illustrated Kids
http://www.sikids.com

INDEX